STOP BEHAVING

A GOSPEL-CENTERED DEVOTIONAL FOR MEN

Written by
JERRAD LOPES

A Dad Tired Resource

JOIN US

Dad Tired is a community
of men from around the world
who are taking their faith, family,
and marriage very seriously.

WWW.DADTIRED.COM

STOP BEHAVING: A DADTIRED.COM RESOURCE

COPYRIGHT © 2017 DAD TIRED MINISTRIES

Author: Jerrad Lopes
Cover Design: Phil Markel
Interior Design: Phil Markel
Editors: Jeannie Wilson & Leila Lopes

ISBN-10: 1944298272
ISBN-13: 978-1944298272

Printed in U.S.A.

WWW.DADTIRED.COM

DEDICATION

TO THE HUMBLE MEN OF THE DAD TIRED COMMUNITY

SHARE YOUR JOURNEY THROUGH THIS DEVOTIONAL USING THE HASHTAG

#DADTIRED

CONTENTS

HOW TO USE THIS BOOK   **5**

Introduction
QUIT YOUR ACCOUNTABILITY GROUP   **7**

Week One
THE GOSPEL & YOUR HEART   **11**

DAY ONE // SALT WATER
DAY TWO // OCEAN FLOOR
DAY THREE // COMMUNITY TABLE
DAY FOUR // TURN DOWN THE RADIO
DAY FIVE // GET HUNGRY
DAY SIX // GET TOGETHER
DAY SEVEN // REST

Week Two
THE GOSPEL & YOUR MARRIAGE   **75**

DAY ONE // HOLY HELPERS
DAY TWO // JUST CAMPING
DAY THREE // BROKEN BRIDES
DAY FOUR // EVERY. SINGLE. DAY.
DAY FIVE // HERE AND NOW
DAY SIX // GET TOGETHER
DAY SEVEN // REST

Week Three
THE GOSPEL & YOUR KIDS   **139**

DAY ONE // A BETTER DAD
DAY TWO // I'M SORRY
DAY THREE // WELL BEHAVED
DAY FOUR // BEAUTIFUL FEET
DAY FIVE // ALIENS
DAY SIX // GET TOGETHER
DAY SEVEN // REST

Week Four
THE GOSPEL & YOUR WORK   **203**

DAY ONE // BUSINESS CARDS
DAY TWO // THE REAL PROVIDER
DAY THREE // GOLD COINS
DAY FOUR // SAY NO MORE
DAY FIVE // PAID MISSIONARIES
DAY SIX // GET TOGETHER
DAY SEVEN // REST

A VIDEO INTRODUCTION FOR EACH WEEK CAN BE FOUND AT

WWW.DADTIRED.COM/VIDEO

HOW TO USE THIS BOOK

DAY ONE-FIVE // LEARN

Read through one chapter each day. Write out any specific prayers
or thoughts that come to mind.

DAY SIX // GATHER

Meet up with some friends who are also going through the book. There
are questions at the end of each week to help keep the conversation
flowing. Talk about what you've learned and how it applies to your life.

DAY SEVEN // REST

Don't skip this part. Resting reminds us that we are saved by the work
of Christ, not our own. I've intentionally left one day open each week
for you to sit and remember what Jesus has done on your behalf. Spend
time reflecting on what you've learned and how it affects your life.
Thank God for saving you by his grace, not by your good behavior.

WHAT'S ON YOUR MIND?

There are no right answers for this page. Write down everything that
comes to mind when you read the chapter. Don't overthink it. This is
a good place to list specific changes that you feel need to be made in
your own life.

PRAYERS

Use this page to write out specific prayers for your heart, your wife,
your kids, and your work.

INTRODUCTION
QUIT YOUR ACCOUNTABILITY GROUP

If you've been around the church world for a while, you've probably been told that you need to join an accountability group. These groups are typically made up of 3 to 5 guys that meet once a week and check in on each other's behavior.

Did you lust?

Did you look at porn?

Did you cuss?

Did you lose your temper?

Years ago, as a young pastor on staff at a church, I was part of a mandatory accountability group with some of the other pastors. During one of our times together, one of the pastors asked me bluntly, "Are you having sex with your girlfriend?" Fortunately I wasn't, so I could honestly answer him with a quick, "No!" But it was still awkward, to say the least.

The whole session lasted about 10 minutes before we quickly moved on to lighter topics.

I understand the point of accountability groups—we want to be the best men that we can be, and we know that if someone else is going to ask us hard questions, we are less likely to do dumb things.

There is just one major problem—accountability groups almost always address the behavior, and very rarely deal with the heart.

Jesus dealt with the exact same problem during his time here on Earth. The religious leaders of his day, called the Pharisees, loved trying to manage the behavior of the people who wanted to follow God. They loved rules. So much so, in fact, that they added their own set of rules to the list of things God had already instructed them to do. The more they followed the rules and managed their behavior, the more righteous they felt.

Jesus was clearly more concerned with a person's heart than their behavior. During one of his teachings, he told the religious leaders that if a person had lusted after a woman, then they had already committed adultery in their heart. Or that if they had hated someone, that they were already guilty of murder. On one occasion, he called them "whitewashed tombs," saying that they looked clean on the outside, but that their hearts were wicked (Matthew 23:27).

This book is not meant to manage your behavior. Behavior management is exhausting and only leads to pride or shame. It leads to pride when you are disciplined enough to follow the "rules" and begin to convince yourself that you're a better Christian than the rest of us. Or, it leads to shame when you, like many of us, screw up over and over again. Jesus wants to free you from both your pride and your shame. You don't need behavior management. You don't need more rules to follow. You need Jesus to change your heart. I'm convinced that if I can point you toward Jesus, and if you are willing to humble yourself enough to draw near to him, that he can, and will, change your heart. And, according to Jesus, a changed heart is the source of changed behavior.

Instead of an accountability group, team up with some guys who can point you toward Jesus and remind you of the Gospel. The group's intention should be to ask "why," not "what." Ask questions that address the heart, not the behavior.

"Why do you feel compelled to look at porn?"

"Why do you want to over-work and neglect your family?"

"Why did you lose your temper?"

My prayer for you is that as you seek Jesus during these next 28 days, you will find him in ways you never have. I pray that you will be released from the heavy burden of behavior modification and will begin to walk freely in the overwhelming grace of Jesus Christ.

THE GOSPEL & YOUR HEART

SALT WATER

SET YOUR MINDS ON THINGS THAT ARE ABOVE. NOT ON THINGS THAT ARE ON EARTH.

COLOSSIANS 3:2

You and I struggle with the exact same sin. In fact, we struggle with the exact same sin that Adam and Eve dealt with in the Garden of Eden.

Before sin had entered into the world, Adam and Eve were perfectly satisfied in God, and God alone. He was the source of their joy, hope, adventure, longing, and fulfillment. They had never experienced joy outside of him.

That is, until the one who was "more crafty than the others" posed a very simple but earth-shattering proposition to Eve:

"For God knows that when you eat of it (the apple) your eyes will be opened, and you will be like God, knowing good and evil." (Genesis 3:5)

It was never about an apple.

Satan wasn't tempting Eve with an apple; he was tempting her with satisfaction outside of God.

The serpent that tempted Eve in the garden is the same enemy that temps you and me today. And although his tactics tend to be extremely effective, they certainly aren't new. The question he planted in Eve's head is the same question that you and I struggle with today:

Is there something other than God that can satisfy my soul?

Imagine you were on a raft, stranded in the middle of the ocean. After two long days of waiting for help to arrive, you become dehydrated to the point of hallucination. You look all around you at the bright blue water, and despite what you know to be true, you decide to start drinking it. At first, you are totally happy with your decision; your thirst is quenched. The cold water is salty, but relieving to your parched mouth. For a second, you are satisfied. But it doesn't take long to realize the terrible decision you've made. What started out as a satisfying drink actually left you more thirsty. And despite everything you know about drinking salt water, your desire to be satisfied pushes you to drink again. If you aren't rescued soon, the salt water will actually kill you.

Like Eve, we are searching for satisfaction outside of Jesus. We are drinking salt water.

Sure, being affirmed at work satisfies for a minute. But it leaves you wanting more. The same is true for porn, and money, and alcohol, and affairs, or whatever else. It always leaves you wanting more.

Remember, we are not chasing after changed behavior, but after a heart that has been changed by Jesus. Our goal is not simply to ask, "Is this right or wrong?" but rather, "Will this satisfy my soul more than Jesus can?"

Brother, there is only one who can satisfy your soul.

As you go throughout your day today, look for all the ways that you are chasing after satisfaction. Where are you searching for joy outside of Jesus? What are you hoping will satisfy your soul, but will ultimately leave you wanting more?

> *Satan wasn't tempting Eve with an apple; he was tempting her with satisfaction outside of God.*

WHAT'S ON YOUR MIND?

PRAYERS FOR YOUR HEART

_____

_____

_____

_____

_____

_____

_____

_____

_____

_____

_____

_____

_____

_____

_____

_____

_____

_____

_____

_____

_____

OCEAN FLOOR

FOR IT IS BY GRACE YOU HAVE BEEN SAVED, THROUGH FAITH—AND THIS IS NOT FROM YOURSELVES, IT IS THE GIFT OF GOD—NOT BY WORKS, SO THAT NO ONE CAN BOAST.

EPHESIANS 2:8-9

How do you go about having your heart changed by God? Unfortunately, there is no magic formula, or some 12-step process that I can walk you through that would guarantee heart change.

For most of us, when we think about wanting to feel closer to God, we typically think about working harder on spiritual disciplines: waking up at 5 am to do your devotional, setting aside time to pray and read your Bible, and listening to a lot more K-LOVE.

Don't get me wrong, these really are great practices, and the last thing I want to do is discourage you from pursuing spiritual disciplines. But at the end of the day, your works will not bring you closer to Jesus—only his grace can do that.

There are two major schools of thought when it comes to salvation in Christ. They are best explained through these analogies:

The first illustrates that you are drowning in the ocean and Jesus pulls up on a lifeboat. He tosses you a life vest and tells you that your only job is to grab it by faith. If you trust in him, you will be saved.

The second says that you drowned in the ocean. Your dead body slowly sinks to the bottom. Jesus pulls up in a lifeboat, jumps in the water, grabs you from the bottom of the ocean, brings you back up to the surface and then breathes life back into your lungs. You didn't do anything to be saved; He did all the work.

I am convinced that the scriptures are clear that we are saved by grace, not by our good works. Listen to what Paul tells the readers of Ephesians: "For it is by grace you have been saved, through faith— and this is not from yourselves, it is the gift of God—not by works, so that no one can boast" (Ephesians 2:8-9).

Brother, you are both saved by grace and sustained by grace. It was his grace that brought you near to him, and it's his grace that will keep you close to him. You didn't do anything to earn or deserve it; he simply was gracious toward you.

Before you commit to practicing spiritual disciplines (which I suggest you do), I encourage you first to have the humility to ask God to draw you near to himself.

> *You are both saved by grace and sustained by grace. It was his grace that brought you near to him, and it's his grace that will keep you close to him.*

WHAT'S ON YOUR MIND?

_____

_____

_____

_____

_____

_____

_____

_____

_____

_____

_____

_____

_____

_____

_____

_____

_____

_____

_____

_____

_____

PRAYERS FOR YOUR HEART

COMMUNITY TABLE

AND LET US CONSIDER HOW TO STIR UP ONE ANOTHER TO LOVE AND GOOD WORKS, NOT NEGLECTING TO MEET TOGETHER, AS IS THE HABIT OF SOME, BUT ENCOURAGING ONE ANOTHER, AND ALL THE MORE AS YOU SEE THE DAY DRAWING NEAR.

HEBREWS 10:24-25

 #DadTired

When Adam and Eve committed humanity's very first sin, their gut-reaction was to run and hide from God. In their shame, they immediately wanted to withdraw from his presence.

If you have kids, you've likely seen the same scenario play out in your own home. After my five-year-old son pushes his younger sister or sneaks a piece of candy from the pantry, he can typically be found hiding shamefully in his room.

Similarly, when we feel burdened by our guilt, we often find ourselves in isolation and feel far from God.

Last year, our family had a goal to host 100 people in our home for a meal. We didn't do this because we are great cooks or even exceptional hosts, but because we knew we needed to be around people more. We knew that by ourselves, we are prone to drift from God.

As people sat at our dinner table each week for a meal, we cried as we heard stories of great faith in the midst of tragedy. We also laughed until we cried as we shared stories of God's goodness. Seeing and hearing the multitude of stories from other people's lives showed us things about God's character that we would have missed if we were in isolation.

In isolation, we lose sight of God's overarching story of redemption and become susceptible to believe the lies of the enemy. We can quickly become convinced that we are the center of God's story and forget that he is at work not just in our lives, but in the lives of those around us.

God, in his very nature, is the greatest example of community. God the Father, Jesus, and the Holy Spirit are perfectly distinct and yet one, enjoying the perfect community and relationship of each other. In the same way, he hardwired us to be in community with each another.

Because we are born sinful, we don't naturally drift toward God; we drift away from him. Left alone for five minutes, five days, or five months, you will likely find yourself far from God. You and I need constant reminders of the Gospel. We need people to remind us of who God is, who he says we are, and what he is doing around the world.

> *In isolation, we lose sight of God's overarching story of redemption and become susceptible to believe the lies of the enemy.*

WHAT'S ON YOUR MIND?

PRAYERS FOR YOUR HEART

TURN DOWN THE RADIO

BUT THE HELPER, THE HOLY SPIRIT, WHOM THE FATHER WILL SEND IN MY NAME, HE WILL TEACH YOU ALL THINGS AND BRING TO YOUR REMEMBERANCE ALL THAT I HAVE SAID TO YOU.

JOHN 14:26

A friend once told me that whenever her car started to make weird noises that might indicate something wrong with the engine, she would simply turn up the radio to drown out the noise.

We are often guilty of doing the same in our spiritual lives.

When something is unsettled in our heart, we do whatever we can to mask it—work harder, drink more, yell louder, buy something new— anything to cover up the noise of our soul. We are convinced that if we can make enough noise, the tugging of the Holy Spirit will go away.

At the root of our noise-making efforts is shame. Shame of what we know will be uncovered when things get quiet—a sinful heart. And the truth is, you're right. Your heart is sinful and wicked, deserving of punishment and shame.

But there is good news. The Gospel.

Jesus said in John 3 that he didn't come to condemn the world, but to save it. He is the only one that has the ability to actually fix your heart. And like Jesus, if we want to experience a heart that is changed by God, we must be intentional about spending time alone with the Father.

Brother, turn off the radio. Stop working so hard. Set down the bottle. Turn off your phone. Be quiet with the Lord today. Block out time in your calendar to spend in prayer, reflection, and worship. Clear away the noise, chaos, and distraction so you can hear the Holy Spirit speak truth into areas of your heart that desperately need him.

It's in the quiet that you can experience grace and freedom from shame. It's in the quiet that you will hear the Holy Spirit, the Reminder (John 14:26), reminding you of who you are in Christ. Yes, the engine is broken, and often times will make noises that we don't want to hear. But we serve the God who makes all things new, the One who can restore all things back to the way they were designed to be.

God has a reputation of restoring broken and messy people. You don't need to mask the noise of your shame anymore.

> **God has a reputation of restoring broken and messy people.**

WHAT'S ON YOUR MIND?

PRAYERS FOR YOUR HEART

GET HUNGRY

KNOW THIS, MY BELOVED BROTHERS: LET EVERY PERSON BE QUICK TO HEAR, SLOW TO SPEAK, SLOW TO ANGER; FOR THE ANGER OF MAN DOES NOT PRODUCE THE RIGHTEOUSNESS OF GOD.

JAMES 1:19-20

 #DadTired

A few years back, while Leila and I were anxiously awaiting the birth of our first son, I decided to take my big-bellied, eight-month-pregnant wife on a romantic date. On our way to dinner, a man passed us in his old pickup truck going about 80 mph. He swerved into our lane and missed hitting the front of our car by about six inches. Normally I would have just let it go, but I had precious cargo riding with me. And it made me mad.

Really mad.

Without even hesitating, I pulled right beside his truck. We made eye contact, and as my blood boiled, I proudly gave him the middle finger. It was less of a decision and more of a reaction.

In Matthew 4, the scriptures tell us that Jesus was led out to the wilderness by the Holy Spirit to be tempted by Satan. This passage is particularly important because the rest of Jesus' ministry depended on how he would respond to this temptation. It's the Garden of Eden scene being played out all over again. And so Jesus prepared himself.

How?

By fasting.

We are all instinctual creatures. When we are hungry, we eat. When we are tired, we sleep. When we see something appealing, we lust. And when we are angry at someone, we pull beside their truck and flip them off. It's instinct.

Forty days after Jesus had been fasting in the desert, Satan shows up. And he tempts him, with food, of course.

Here is how Jesus responds:

"'Man shall not live by bread alone, but by every word that comes from the mouth of God'" (Matthew 4:4).

It's interesting that when Jesus knows he will be faced with temptation, he decides to fast. He allows his flesh to be weak so that the Spirit in him will be strong.

Like Jesus, you and I will be tempted.

Daily.

Hourly.

Obedience to Jesus today means not living by bread alone, but by the Word of God. What would it look like for you not to simply live by human instinct, but rather by the Word and Spirit of God? What if instead of eating when you're hungry, you say "no"? Practice saying no to your flesh and allow the Spirit of God in you to have a louder voice.

Fasting is really just practice; it is less about the food and more about the discipline of saying no to the reactions of your flesh. You don't have to eat when you're hungry. You also don't have to lust when you see something you like. You don't have to yell at your wife or kids when you're angry. You don't have to flip a guy off when he almost crashes into your car. And you don't have to fall into temptation when Satan tempts you.

Obedience to Jesus today means not living by bread alone, but by the Word of God.

WHAT'S ON YOUR MIND?

PRAYERS FOR YOUR HEART

_____

_____

_____

_____

_____

_____

_____

_____

_____

_____

_____

_____

_____

_____

_____

_____

_____

_____

_____

WEEK ONE // DAY SIX

GET TOGETHER

We'd love to see who you're meeting with. Post a picture of your group and use the hashtag **#DadTired**.

MEET WITH SOME FRIENDS OVER FOOD AND DRINK TO TALK ABOUT WHAT YOU LEARNED THIS WEEK. USE THESE QUESTIONS TO HELP KEEP THE CONVERSATION GOING.

What things are you currently chasing after to bring you joy, satisfaction, and comfort outside of Jesus?

Do you have a hard time believing that you don't need to earn God's grace? Why or why not?

What about your upbringing or life-events has led you to believe that love and grace are based on how well you behave?

Who are the people in your life that point you toward Jesus?

What would it look like to be more intentional with those people?

What practical changes would you need to make in order to spend more time alone with God?

In what situations do you find yourself reacting on impulse?

In what ways do you currently deal with temptation? What are your thoughts on fasting?

REST

#DadTired

BUT YOU ARE A CHOSEN RACE, A ROYAL PRIESTHOOD, A HOLY NATION, A PEOPLE FOR HIS OWN POSSESSION, THAT YOU MAY PROCLAIM THE EXCELLENCIES OF HIM WHO CALLED YOU OUT OF DARKNESS INTO HIS MARVELOUS LIGHT. ONCE YOU WERE NOT A PEOPLE, BUT NOW YOU ARE GOD'S PEOPLE; ONCE YOU HAD NOT RECEIVED MERCY, BUT NOW YOU HAVE RECEIVED MERCY.

1 PETER 2:9-10

WHAT'S ON YOUR MIND?

PRAYERS FOR YOUR HEART

_____

_____

_____

_____

_____

_____

_____

_____

_____

_____

_____

_____

_____

_____

_____

_____

_____

THE GOSPEL & YOUR MARRIAGE

WEEK TWO // DAY ONE

HOLY HELPERS

HE WHO FINDS A WIFE FINDS A GOOD THING AND OBTAINS FAVOR FROM THE LORD.

PROVERBS 18:22

 #DadTired

It's not hard to spot the difference between most newlywed couples and those couples who have been married for several years.

Proverbs 18:22 says, "He who finds a wife finds a good thing and obtains favor from the LORD."

A newly married or newly engaged man is obviously convinced that he is favored by God and has certainly found a good thing. He walks around with extra pep in his step and a smile that is constantly stuck to his happy-go-lucky face.

Sadly, the same can't be said for most men who have experienced the battlefield of marriage. I've sat across from dozens, if not hundreds of men who have grown bitter toward the woman that was once the source of their beaming joy.

How does this happen? How does a man go from feeling favored by God to questioning why God would give him such a difficult woman?

It starts with the premise.

Let's go back to the beginning and look at the very first married couple—Adam and Eve.

At the beginning of creation, we see God take great pride in his creative work. He created galaxies, oceans, forests, and wildlife, and after each day, the scriptures tell us that he looked at his creation and "saw that it was good." In fact, after creating his most prized possession, Adam, God exclaimed, "It is very good."

And then God said something very interesting.

"It is not good that man should be alone; I will make a helper fit for him."

It's the very first time in scripture that we see God say something isn't good. There was no sin, no shame, no condemnation, and yet, Adam's "aloneness" still wasn't good. God had something better in mind.

Notice that God didn't create a "best friend" for Adam; he created a helper.

Fast forward thousands of years and God is still creating helpers for men. He is not creating soul mates, best friends, or "other halves," he is creating helpers.

Brother, your wife was designed for your holiness, not your happiness. In God's sovereignty, he gave you a helper who would not necessarily be like you, but who would help shape you into the man that he desires you to be.

When the premise of our marriage is happiness, we will quickly find ourselves bitter toward our wife when she stops producing joy in us. Be reminded, her role is not to be the source of your joy, but rather, to be

God's uniquely designed partner for your growth. When we begin to see our wife as the gift God has given us for our sanctification, we will start to resonate deeply with James' words, "Count it all joy, my brothers, when you meet trials of various kinds, for you know that the testing of your faith produces steadfastness. And let steadfastness have its full effect, that you may be perfect and complete, lacking in nothing" (James 1:2).

> *Your wife was designed for your holiness, not your happiness.*

WHAT'S ON YOUR MIND?

PRAYERS FOR YOUR MARRIAGE

JUST CAMPING

BUT OUR CITIZENSHIP IS IN HEAVEN, AND FROM IT WE AWAIT OUR SAVIOR, THE LORD JESUS CHRIST.

PHILIPPIANS 3:20

When I was a kid, my mom used to take us camping each year. The week before our trip, she would take some time off work so that we could properly prepare. It was a big deal. Somehow she managed to pack our little Volkswagen Jetta with ice chests, tents, sleeping bags, portable showers, cooking utensils, and who knows what else. The neighbors were always convinced that we were moving.

But we weren't. We were just camping. And despite the fact that the amount of gear could very well have indicated that we may never return, we always did—usually just two days later. While packing day was always exciting and brimming with anticipation, the return trip home and unpacking felt silly. We spent so much time, money, and effort for just two days of camping.

In one of his letters to the Church, Peter called his readers "sojourners," reminding them that Earth is not their home, but simply a place that they are passing through (1 Peter 2:11). In the book of Philippians, Paul makes it even more clear—"But our citizenship is in heaven, and from it we await our Savior, the Lord Jesus Christ" (Philippians 3:20).

We're just camping.

Our time on Earth is the shortest amount of time we will spend anywhere. Even if you are blessed with a long life, well into your nineties, it pales in comparison to the infinite years you will spend in eternity.

Christian marriages will always find themselves in trouble when they begin to lose sight of this reality. Things like money, sex, food, childcare, and the size of a house will start to feel like bigger problems than they actually are. When a couple forgets that God has brought them together for the advancement of his Kingdom, they will become passionate about trivial things instead of the things that will last for eternity. They are packing for a camping trip on Earth instead of storing up treasures for eternity.

When you begin to view life through the lens of eternity, remembering that this place is not your home, you start to become the husband God desires you to be. Instead of becoming passionate about work, sports, or the size of your TV, you will become passionate about leading your wife toward things that will have an eternal impact.

Brother, this world is not your home. You are simply passing through. What problems are you currently facing that might seem silly in light of eternity? In what areas of your life are you spending too much time that will have no impact on the Kingdom of God? In what ways could you and your wife use your time, talent, and money to make a difference that will last forever?

"When a couple forgets that God has brought them together for the advancement of his Kingdom, they will become passionate about trivial things instead of the things that will last for eternity."

WHAT'S ON YOUR MIND?

PRAYERS FOR YOUR MARRIAGE

BROKEN BRIDES

I WILL MAKE YOU MY WIFE FOREVER, SHOWING YOU RIGHTEOUSNESS AND JUSTICE, UNFAILING LOVE AND COMPASSION. I WILL BE FAITHFUL TO YOU AND MAKE YOU MINE, AND YOU WILL FINALLY KNOW ME AS THE LORD.

HOSEA 2:19-20 (NLT)

#DadTired

God didn't save you because you're awesome. He saved you because he's awesome.

The entire Old Testament tells the story of God pursuing the Israelites, despite their unfaithfulness to him. One of the most beautiful, and humbling, summaries of this story can be found in the book of Hosea. The book starts off describing the broken marriage of Hosea and his wife Gomer—a prostitute. Though married, Gomer repeatedly commits adultery and is unfaithful to her husband. Hosea had every right to leave, but God tells him to remain faithful to her, despite her unfaithfulness. He then tells Hosea that the whole point of their marriage is to symbolize God's faithfulness to an unfaithful Israel. Despite their behavior and lack of commitment, God didn't bail.

God compared Hosea and Gomer's broken, earthly marriage to his relationship with the people of the Old Testament. He later called the church (all followers of Jesus) his "bride." What was true about the Israelites is true about us—we have been an unfaithful bride. And what's most amazing is the fact that God not only remained faithful to the people of the Old Testament, but also remains faithful to us. He still hasn't bailed.

If you are to be the kind of husband that God desires you to be, you must first understand the kind of "bride" that you are. I know that sounds like weird language, but we aren't talking about males and females. We're talking about God and his church. You, his bride, his beloved, are unfaithful. Like Gomer, you and I have run away from God time and time again. We have searched for significance and pleasure outside of Christ. We have been unfaithful. And God hasn't bailed. Not because you are awesome, but because he is awesome.

When you begin to understand that you are the terrible partner, and yet God continues to pursue you, you will then have the motivation to pursue your wife with zero strings attached. You can forgive with unending forgiveness because Jesus forgives you with unending forgiveness. You can show relentless grace because God is relentless in his grace toward you. And you can have unwavering patience because you know that Jesus is unwavering in his patience toward you.

Brother, stop expecting your wife to be a perfect wife. You are not perfect and yet God won't bail on you. Don't forget the grace and forgiveness you have been shown as you continue to show grace and forgiveness to your bride.

You can forgive with unending forgiveness because Jesus forgives you with unending forgiveness.

WHAT'S ON YOUR MIND?

PRAYERS FOR YOUR MARRIAGE

EVERY.
SINGLE.
DAY.

HUSBANDS, LOVE YOUR WIVES, AS CHRIST LOVED THE CHURCH AND GAVE HIMSELF UP FOR HER.

EPHESIANS 5:25

#DadTired

Remember when you first met your wife?

If you're like most guys, you probably did everything you possibly could to try to impress her. Nothing was off limits. She was a mystery that you couldn't wait to explore. You were so excited to learn everything there was to know about her.

And then you got married.

The butterflies fluttered away. The kids were born. The excitement faded. And instead of seeing her as a mystery to be explored, you've become convinced that you have learned everything there is to know about her. You became complacent.

Imagine if God treated us the way we often treat our wife. Imagine that he pursued us once, and then when we "said the prayer" and became a Christian, he stopped chasing our heart.

Some therapists have spent years studying the idea of attachment, or feeling a sense of "oneness" with your spouse. They are finding that this feeling of closeness begins to fade within as little as 24 hours of your last strong connection. This means that you can take your wife on a romantic date or an exotic vacation, and despite feeling on top of the world, your attachment toward each other can begin to fade away almost immediately.

When God led the Israelites out of slavery and through the desert, he would provide enough food for them to last one day. And only one day. In fact, if they tried to hoard enough food for the following day, it would be rotten by morning.

God knew that the Israelites were prone to forget, prone to wander, and prone to become complacent. He set up a system in which they had to depend on him every single day. He didn't want a once a week, once a month, or once a year interaction. He wanted a daily relationship.

God continues to pursue our hearts daily. He didn't save you so that one day you can go to heaven. He saved you so that you can continue to know him and fall in love with him, daily.

And then he tells you to love your wife the same way that he loves you (Ephesians 5:25).

You are literally hard-wired to chase after the heart of your wife every single day. Once a week, once a month, or once a year dates won't suffice. You must pursue her heart every day. Brother, God is relentless in his pursuit of your heart. May you be the same toward your wife.

> *God is relentless in his pursuit of your heart. May you be the same toward your wife.*

WHAT'S ON YOUR MIND?

PRAYERS FOR YOUR MARRIAGE

_____

_____

_____

_____

_____

_____

_____

_____

_____

_____

_____

_____

_____

_____

_____

_____

_____

_____

_____

_____

_____

_____

_____

HERE AND NOW

YOUR KINGDOM COME, YOUR WILL BE DONE, ON EARTH AS IT IS IN HEAVEN.

MATTHEW 6:10

 #DadTired

When Jesus was teaching his disciples how to pray, he instructed them to ask that God's Kingdom would come and that his will would be done, on Earth as it is in Heaven (Matthew 6:10).

Jesus told his disciples that the Kingdom of God isn't just a "one day" thing that would happen in the future. He taught them that it can also be experienced today, in the here and now. The culture of Heaven, the way The King operates, can be seen in the normal everyday stuff of life.

If you and your wife are followers of Jesus, you have the opportunity to be used by God to see pieces of Heaven come here to Earth. God desires to use your marriage not simply for your joy, but for the advancement of his Kingdom. He can use you, and your marriage, to show off what Heaven is like to the rest of the world.

I often meet couples that are confused about how they can be used radically by God, and they typically settle for much less than what God designed for them. They rarely take the time to seek out how God has designed and paired them uniquely for his glory. As a result, they end up feeling burned out or used by the church.

What if God has more in store for your marriage than to volunteer on Sundays? Don't get me wrong, we should be faithful to serve in our local church and not just consume from it. But what if God has more for you? What if your unique personalities, style, relationship and passions were given to you for a bigger purpose? What if God was intentional about bringing you and your wife together so that he could use you in unique and powerful ways to advance his story of redemption?

My wife and I have a mission statement for our marriage and home:

"Our mission is to see every person drawn a little bit closer to Jesus than when they first walked through our front door."

We believe that God has wired us in such a way as to host and make people feel comfortable in our home. We could use that gift simply to throw a lot of parties for friends, or we could use it intentionally to see the Kingdom of God advance. For every person that walks into our house, we know that God wants to use us in our unique gifting to draw people back to himself.

How has God uniquely wired your marriage to do the same? Are you active and enjoy the outdoors? Are you good at hosting and loving on people in your home? Does your marriage embody compassion toward the vulnerable? Regardless of how you are wired, God wants to use your marriage to see his Kingdom come and his will be done on Earth as it is in Heaven.

God wants to use your marriage to see his Kingdom come and his will be done on Earth as it is in Heaven.

WHAT'S ON YOUR MIND?

PRAYERS FOR YOUR MARRIAGE

GET TOGETHER

MEET WITH SOME FRIENDS OVER FOOD AND DRINK TO TALK ABOUT WHAT YOU LEARNED THIS WEEK. USE THESE QUESTIONS TO HELP KEEP THE CONVERSATION GOING.

What qualities does your wife have that you don't? What are her areas of strength that can help you grow?

Are there issues in your marriage that would feel less significant if you were thinking in light of eternity?

What emotions do you feel when you think about God's faithfulness toward you, despite not being faithful to him?

How does this change the way you relate to your wife?

What stops you from pursuing your wife every single day?

What things could you do to be more intentional in your pursuit of her heart?

If you could dream about being used by God in big ways to see his Kingdom come to Earth, what would be some things you'd do as a married couple?

WEEK TWO // DAY SEVEN

REST

#DadTired

WHOEVER WOULD
SAVE HIS LIFE
WILL LOSE IT,
BUT WHOEVER
LOSES HIS LIFE
FOR MY SAKE
AND THE GOSPEL'S
WILL SAVE IT.

MARK 8:35

WHAT'S ON YOUR MIND?

PRAYERS FOR YOUR MARRIAGE

THE GOSPEL & YOUR KIDS

A BETTER DAD

FOR YOU DID NOT RECEIVE THE SPIRIT OF SLAVERY TO FALL BACK INTO FEAR, BUT YOU HAVE RECEIEVED THE SPIRIT OF ADOPTION AS SONS, BY WHOM WE CRY 'ABBA! FATHER!'

ROMANS 8:15

 #DadTired

Most of us want to be a better dad than our dad was to us. I've met a few rare exceptions of guys who absolutely adore everything about their father. But for the most part, the majority of us are striving to give their children a better childhood experience than they had.

There is nothing wrong with that. Your desire to give "good gifts" to your kids is much like God's heart to care for his children. There is just one problem.

You are a terrible god.

In your longing to be the best father that you can be, you will likely set standards for yourself that are impossible to maintain. As much as you want to be the dad who has all the patience in the world, you will eventually lose your temper. You may have grand intentions of giving your kids all your time and energy, but you will eventually become exhausted and need a break.

The good news is that God never expected you to be a perfect father. But he does expect that you would point your kids to the one who is. Your goal isn't to be the best dad in the world, or even to be better than your dad was. Your goal should be to point your kids to the only one who can actually satisfy their soul.

Every morning as I drive my kids to school, I pray over them and purposely use the same words that Jesus used when he was teaching his disciples how to pray. All of my prayers start with:

"God, you are such a good daddy..."

Jesus wanted his disciples to be convinced fully that because of the Gospel, they could relate to God in a way that no other human could relate to any other god. Jesus was teaching them that God wasn't just majestic, or almighty, or all-powerful, or Lord of their life. He is also "Abba." He is daddy.

Brother, you don't have to carry the pressure of being a perfect dad. Instead, point your kids to the one who already is the perfect father. Point your kids to the one who will always give his attention to your children. Point them to the one who never gets exhausted. Point them to the one who never loses his temper. Point them to the one who never grows tired of extending grace and forgiveness.

There is nothing more valuable that you can give your kids than to remind them that both you and they serve the best daddy.

You don't have to carry the pressure of being a perfect dad. Instead, point your kids to the one who already is the perfect father.

WHAT'S ON YOUR MIND?

PRAYERS FOR YOUR KIDS

I'M SORRY

IF WE CONFESS OUR SINS, HE IS FAITHFUL AND JUST TO FORGIVE US OUR SINS AND TO CLEANSE US FROM ALL UNRIGHTEOUSNESS.

1 JOHN 1:9

#DadTired

At its core, the Gospel of Jesus is this: We are all screwed up and in need of serious grace. And instead of God bailing on us, leaving us in our mess, he instead pursues and rescues us.

This is good news.

But it's only good news when we realize that we actually need grace. That we fall short all the time. That we can never be perfect, no matter how hard we try. In fact, the more we realize how jacked up we are, the more amazing that grace becomes.

As dads, here is where we can really confuse our kids:

Somehow we convince ourselves that we need to be the "know-it-all" of the family. The guy who fixes everything and has the answer to every problem. The guy who doesn't mess up.

And then, as a Christian dad, you try to teach your kids that they are in need of grace and should turn to Jesus for forgiveness. Yet, they've never seen you do that. They've never heard the words "I'm sorry" come from your mouth. They have no context or model of seeking forgiveness because they have never seen dad admit to his failures and ask for forgiveness.

In many ways, you are modeling a contradiction—that if always being right is a sign of strength, you are asking your kids to be weak by turning to Jesus for forgiveness.

Saying the words "I'm sorry," and saying them often, models to our kids that it's okay to fall short. It demonstrates that there is grace beyond our shortcomings, and no one is expected to be perfect. It's this type of fathering that will make the Good News of Jesus easier to understand when our children one day recognize their own junk and turn to the Father for grace. They will be able to do it with both humility and confidence, because they've seen their daddy do it time and time again.

Modeling strength for our kids, especially our boys, is not teaching them to have all the right answers. We model strength when we have the courage to say, "I'm sorry. I wronged you and I'd like to ask for your forgiveness."

Humility takes much more strength than pride.

When you fail your kids, apologize. When you fail your wife, let your kids see you ask her for forgiveness. By doing this, you are actually planting Gospel seeds in their hearts, well before they can even fully understand the Good News.

> *We model strength to our kids when we have the courage to say, 'I'm sorry.'*

WHAT'S ON YOUR MIND?

PRAYERS FOR YOUR KIDS

_____

_____

_____

_____

_____

_____

_____

_____

_____

_____

_____

_____

_____

_____

_____

_____

_____

_____

_____

_____

WELL BEHAVED

THE GOOD PERSON OUT OF THE GOOD TREASURE OF HIS HEART PRODUCES GOOD, AND THE EVIL PERSON OUT OF HIS EVIL TREASURE PRODUCES EVIL, FOR OUT OF THE ABUNDANCE OF THE HEART HIS MOUTH SPEAKS.

LUKE 6:45

Your kids are just like you and me—they don't have behavior issues, they have heart issues. Behavior is always an overflow of the heart.

"...for out of the abundance of the heart his mouth speaks" (Luke 6:45).

Jesus had a way of getting to the heart of any issue. If anyone had the right to tell people how to behave, it was Jesus. He was the only perfect human ever to walk the earth and the only one qualified to judge the behavior of another person. And yet, he didn't try to manage behavior, but instead, realign hearts. Jesus understood that there was always a why behind the what. In other words, what someone did was not as much the issue as why they did it.

There is a story in the Bible of Jesus encountering an adulterous woman while he was getting some water. This woman hadn't just cheated on her husband once, but multiple times, and Jesus knew about it. Instead of shaming her behavior, he spoke right to her heart. He knew that her soul was thirsty and unsatisfied, and therefore was turning to other men to get her needs met. Listen to his response:

"Everyone who drinks of this water will be thirsty again, but whoever drinks of the water that I will give him will never be thirsty again. The water that I will give him will become in him a spring of water welling up to eternal life." (John 4:13-14)

Jesus wasn't talking about water. He was talking about himself. He is the living water that causes our soul never to thirst again. He wasn't telling this adulterous woman simply to manage her behavior. He was pointing her to the only thing that could actually satisfy her soul—himself.

It's easy for us to want to manage the behavior of our children. When they don't listen to our instructions, when they complain about not having the latest toy, when they throw a tantrum in the middle of the store, we want nothing more than for their behavior to change. But poor behavior is simply a glimpse into your child's heart.

As Christian fathers, we are not trying to raise well-behaved children. We are trying to raise children who find satisfaction in Jesus above all else. The next time your child misbehaves or throws a tantrum, ask yourself what is the "why" behind the action. What is happening deep inside her heart? Most likely, she is chasing after something or someone to give her satisfaction outside of Jesus. They are worshipping a god that will fail them (food, friends, games, sports, money, clothes, etc.). Point them to a better God. Point their hearts toward Jesus.

> *Poor behavior is simply a glimpse into your child's heart.*

WHAT'S ON YOUR MIND?

PRAYERS FOR YOUR KIDS

BEAUTIFUL FEET

HOW BEAUTIFUL ARE THE FEET OF THOSE WHO PREACH THE GOOD NEWS!

ROMANS 10:15

Do you have beautiful feet?

If you're like the majority of men, the answer is probably no.

In the book of Romans, Paul makes an interesting comment about feet to his readers. Take a look:

"How beautiful are the feet of those who preach the good news!" (Romans 10:15).

But what exactly is the good news that Paul is referring to?

The Good News of Jesus is that God didn't bail on us. We were broken, rebellious, sinful people, and yet, instead of God running away from us, he ran toward us. Instead of him giving us the punishment that we deserved, he gave us mercy. Instead of him calling us his forever enemies, he called us his forever children. God doesn't hate us, or even just tolerate us—he delights in us.

That's really good news.

Such good news, in fact, that it changes every aspect of our lives. It allows us to find hope in hopeless situations. It allows us to set down our anxiety because we know that there is a God who loves us and who is in control. It allows us to set aside our fear of politics, war, and even death, because we know that our eternity is secured with God.

It's because of this good news that the writer of Psalm 13:5 can say, "But I have trusted in your steadfast love; my heart shall rejoice in your salvation." We have been given the greatest news of all time, and it is the source of our joy.

Would your kids describe you as the giver of good news? When they look at your life (and trust me, they are looking), do they see a man who has been affected by this good news? Do they see a man who has joy from his salvation (Psalm 51:12)?

As dads, we take seriously our role as protector, provider, and enforcer, but often forget that we are the primary person responsible for bringing this good news to our kids. When they hear your footsteps approaching, may they be the footsteps of beautiful feet bringing good news.

Brother, don't just be the one who brings rules and discipline to your home. Laugh with your kids. Have fun with them. Enjoy them. Delight in them. Let them see that you have been changed by the greatest news of all time. Live a life that convinces them that there is no greater news on Earth than knowing that the God of all creation delights in both you and them.

Don't just be the one who brings rules and discipline to your home. Laugh with your kids.

WHAT'S ON YOUR MIND?

PRAYERS FOR YOUR KIDS

_____

_____

_____

_____

_____

_____

_____

_____

_____

_____

_____

_____

_____

_____

_____

_____

_____

_____

_____

_____

_____

WEEK THREE // DAY FIVE

ALIENS

BELOVED, I URGE YOU AS SOJOURNERS AND EXILES TO ABSTAIN FROM THE PASSIONS OF THE FLESH, WHICH WAGE WAR AGAINST YOUR SOUL.

1 PETER 2:11

Several years ago, I had the opportunity to travel to Africa to work with some Kenyan pastors. During my stay, one of the pastors asked me if I'd like to go with him to the grocery store, to which I agreed. I'll never forget that experience. As I walked around the store with my new African friend, I felt the eyes of every other person staring directly at me. Apparently it was obvious that I wasn't a local, and my fair skin made me stand out like a sore thumb. I was clearly a foreigner in their land.

In one of his letters to the early Christians, Peter actually calls his readers "aliens and foreigners" of this world (1 Peter 2:11), reminding them that as Christians, this Earth is not their home. Later in the Bible, Paul reminds us that "our citizenship is in heaven, and from it we await a Savior, the Lord Jesus Christ" (Philippians 3:20).

Our citizenship is in the Kingdom of Heaven, and Jesus is our king.

As a Christian father, you won't have to teach your kids about the kingdom of this world—the world has a way of doing that on its own. But, you will have to teach your kids about the Kingdom of Heaven. Your kids, just like you and I, will naturally drift toward the culture of this world, not the culture of Heaven. We are born into sin and prone to wander.

The kingdom of this world will teach your kids how to demand revenge when they are wronged. The Kingdom of Heaven will teach your kids how to forgive the way that Jesus has forgiven them. The kingdom of this world will teach your kids that sex, money, and status will satisfy their soul. The Kingdom of Heaven will teach them that nothing in this world can satisfy their soul like Jesus can.

Being a Gospel-centered dad means using every opportunity to teach your kids about the Kingdom of Heaven and the king we serve. Our goal is not simply to raise moral children, but children who recognize that they are part of a different kingdom and serve a different king. Brother, use every opportunity to point your kids back to the only Kingdom that will last forever.

Being a Gospel-centered dad means using every opportunity to teach your kids about the Kingdom of Heaven.

WHAT'S ON YOUR MIND?

PRAYERS FOR YOUR KIDS

GET TOGETHER

We'd love to see who you're meeting with. Post a
picture of your group and use the hashtag **#DadTired**.

MEET WITH SOME FRIENDS OVER FOOD AND DRINK TO TALK ABOUT WHAT YOU LEARNED THIS WEEK. USE THESE QUESTIONS TO HELP KEEP THE CONVERSATION GOING.

Do you have a hard time relating to God as a Good Father? Why or why not?

Do you have any insecurities when it comes to teaching your kids about God?

Is it hard for you to apologize to your kids when you wrong them? How would apologizing to your kids help them understand the Gospel?

What are some ways that the Kingdom of Heaven is different than the kingdom of Earth?

Think of an issue with which your kids are currently dealing. How could you use that issue to teach them something about the Kingdom, or the culture of God?

WEEK THREE // DAY SEVEN

REST

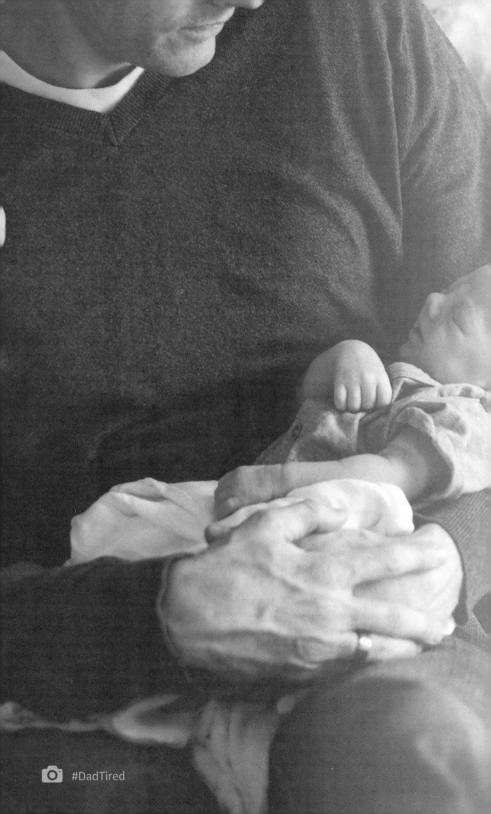
#DadTired

YOU SHALL LOVE THE LORD YOUR GOD WITH ALL YOUR HEART AND WITH ALL YOUR SOUL AND WITH ALL YOUR MIGHT. AND THESE WORDS THAT I COMMAND YOU TODAY SHALL BE ON YOUR HEART. YOU SHALL TEACH THEM DILIGENTLY TO YOUR CHILDREN, AND SHALL TALK OF THEM WHEN YOU SIT IN YOUR HOUSE, AND WHEN YOU WALK BY THE WAY, AND WHEN YOU LIE DOWN, AND WHEN YOU RISE.

DEUTERONOMY 6:4-7

WHAT'S ON YOUR MIND?

PRAYERS FOR YOUR KIDS

THE GOSPEL & YOUR WORK

BUSINESS CARDS

SEE WHAT KIND OF LOVE THE FATHER HAS GIVEN TO US, THAT WE SHOULD BE CALLED CHILDREN OF GOD; AND SO WE ARE.

1 JOHN 3:1

 #DadTired

If I asked a group of men, "Who are you?" the majority would respond with their profession as part of their answer. We have deeply connected who we are with what we do.

A few years back, as I was hanging out with a large number of men in Kenya, one common theme stuck out to me. After introducing myself, the Kenyan men then introduce themselves by saying this:

"Hello, my name is _____, and I've been saved by the grace of Jesus Christ."

I heard this statement so often that it literally became the most impactful part of the trip for me.

Unlike me, their identity wasn't connected to what they did, but rather, to who they were in Christ. They weren't simply carpenters, electricians, or farmers. They were sons of the Most High God. It was the truest thing about them and it impacted every other area of their life.

For the majority of us, the title of "Christian" typically falls low on the list of things that identify us. This truth is most evident when we meet someone new for the first time. Within minutes, the other person knows our name, where we live, what we do for work, and possibly even a bit about our family, but rarely do they learn that we are saved by the grace of Jesus Christ. That reality has yet to consume us and therefore rarely makes it's way into conversation.

As Christian husbands and fathers, we play a dangerous game when we allow anything to shape our identity outside of Christ. By doing this, we will either fall into the temptation of pride, or the unnecessary trap of inadequacy.

On one end of the spectrum we have those who take deep pride in what they do. They are shaped by their work and find great security in their job title. Their confidence comes not from who they are in Christ, but rather, who they are at work. The problem with this way of thinking is that it offers a false sense of security. At any moment, you could lose your job or the economy could collapse. Your hope is not built on the rock of Jesus, but on sinking sand.

On the other hand we have those that feel a sense of inadequacy or worthlessness because they don't have a job in which they take pride. They sheepishly walk around as if their only value comes from the amount of money they make or the job they possess.

Equally dangerous is the fact that when we are not secure in our identity in Christ alone, we begin subtly to project that type of thinking onto our kids. We parent, motivate, and discipline based on performance and therefore subtly teach our kids that their value comes from what they do, not who (or whose) they are.

Brothers, if you are placing your identity in anything other than Jesus, you are destined for failure. That yoke is too heavy. You will succumb to the temptation of pride or the weight of shame. Come back to Jesus.

Take pride instead in your identity in Christ. You have immeasurable value—not based on what you do, but in who Jesus says you are.

He calls you son. He calls you beloved. He calls you his own.

And that is enough.

"You have immeasurable value—not based on what you do, but in who Jesus says you are."

WHAT'S ON YOUR MIND?

PRAYERS FOR YOUR WORK

THE REAL PROVIDER

LOOK AT THE BIRDS OF THE AIR: THEY NEITHER SOW NOR REAP NOR GATHER INTO BARNS, AND YET YOUR HEAVENLY FATHER FEEDS THEM. ARE YOU NOT MORE VALUABLE THAN THEY?

MATTHEW 6:26

 #DadTired

One of the most misunderstood Biblical concepts is a man's role as provider.

I've talked with men in my church who felt like they were failing as provider for their household because they were bringing home less than a hundred thousand dollars per year. I've also talked with Christian men in Africa who wept over the thought of not being able to provide clean water for their children to drink.

Clearly something is wrong.

When speaking to their church, Christian teachers often attempt to encourage men out of laziness by telling them they must be the provider for their family. There is just one major problem with this teaching. The scriptures are overwhelmingly clear about who is the provider, and it's certainly not you or me.

From the first pages of the Bible to the last, we read the story of a God who provides for his people. We learn of a God who provides grace for the wicked, food for the hungry, shelter for the homeless, rest for the weary, safety for the lost, and forgiveness for sinners. There is no other provider like him.

Yes, brother, you should be working hard to help meet the basic needs of your family, of course. But do not confuse your role with God's. Listen to what Jesus told a group of followers on the topic:

"Therefore I tell you, do not be anxious about your life, what you will eat or what you will drink, nor about your body, what you will put on. Is not life more than food, and the body more than clothing? Look at the birds of the air: they neither sow nor reap nor gather into barns, and yet your heavenly Father feeds them. Are you not of more value than they?" (Matthew 6:25-26)

Notice the one who was feeding the birds of the air—God, not us.

Teach your kids that their needs for today have been met, not because their daddy worked extra hard, but because they serve a gracious heavenly Father who is the greatest provider.

Too many men neglect their families under the guise of providing for their family. A Gospel-centered man is not lazy, but humbly gives thanks to God for the mind and body he has given him. A Gospel-centered man recognizes that it is only by God's grace that he is able to contribute to the basic needs of the household. A Gospel-centered man recognizes that provision involves more than money, and he works hard to meet the spiritual, emotional, and financial needs of the household.

" A Gospel-centered man is not lazy, but humbly gives thanks to God for the mind and body he has given him. "

WHAT'S ON YOUR MIND?

PRAYERS FOR YOUR WORK

GOLD COINS

NO ONE CAN SERVE TWO MASTERS, FOR EITHER HE WILL HATE THE ONE AND LOVE THE OTHER, OR HE WILL BE DEVOTED TO THE ONE AND DESPISE THE OTHER. YOU CANNOT SERVE GOD AND MONEY.

MATTHEW 6:24

 #DadTired

Money has a reputation for pretending to be God. In many ways it can appear to be God—it can give you a (false) sense of safety, belonging, value, and even identity. It's no wonder that money is the only thing in scripture to which Jesus ever compared himself.

"No one can serve two masters, for either he will hate the one and love the other, or he will be devoted to the one and despise the other. You cannot serve God and money." (Matthew 6:24)

Nothing on Earth competes with God like money does. Jesus knows the power that money processes, and as a result left no middle ground—"... he will hate the one and love the other..."

When we serve money, there is no need to depend on God as provider if your savings account is full. And there is no need to rest in your identity in Christ when, by serving money, you can rest in your socio-economic status.

Money has power to compete with God, but money is not inherently evil. In fact, despite popular belief, the Bible never says that money is the root of evil. Instead, it talks about the love of money:

"For the love of money is a root of all kinds of evils. It is through this craving that some have wandered away from the faith and pierced themselves with many pangs." (1 Timothy 6:10)

You don't have to be rich to love money. Both the rich and poor have succumbed to the craving that has caused many to wander away from the faith. It is both the rich and the poor that have abandoned their hope in Jesus and instead found hope in finances, both real and hoped for.

Brother, money is a terrible god. It will always leave you unsatisfied and wanting more. It will fail to give you the true hope, safety, and identity for which you are longing.

A Gospel-centered man doesn't crave money, but craves to give God glory with whatever amount of money he does have. Money does not have to be evil, but can instead be used by a Godly man to see the Kingdom of Heaven invade Earth. When used in a righteous way, money has the ability to give food to the hungry, clothes to the naked, and shelter to the homeless.

May we never seek to trade the God of the Universe for a gold coin, but instead, use every dollar we have to point people back to their creator.

A Gospel-centered man doesn't crave money, but craves to give God glory with whatever amount of money he does have.

WHAT'S ON YOUR MIND?

PRAYERS FOR YOUR WORK

WEEK FOUR // DAY FOUR

SAY NO MORE

FOR WHERE YOUR TREASURE IS, THERE YOUR HEART WILL BE ALSO.

MATTHEW 6:21

You likely will have had many job titles in your career by the time you retire. What you do constantly changes, but who you are remains the same.

You are a disciple of Jesus.

You are a husband.

You are a father.

These are the titles that will remain with you until the day you die. They are the greatest titles you could ever hold. The titles of disciple, husband, and father carry more weight than any job you could ever present on a business card.

It's amazing how many of us understand this concept intellectually, but fail to live out its values practically.

We say we love Jesus, but we give more attention to our e-mail inbox than we do our relationships with him. We say we value our marriages, but fail to set down our phones in order to pursue the heart of our wife. We say we would do anything for our kids, but find ourselves more addicted to the accomplishments of work than the accomplishment of raising children who love the Lord.

Our priority lists say one thing, but our calendars prove another.

The scriptures reveal to us how focused of a leader Jesus was. Every word he spoke and every action he took had a purpose. He knew his mission was to seek and save the lost, and he aligned his entire life around it. He spent time on the things that would have the most impact for eternity.

On one occasion, Jesus was so focused on his mission that he wouldn't even be bothered to eat. Take a look:

"Meanwhile the disciples were urging him, saying, 'Rabbi, eat.' But he said to them, 'I have food to eat that you do not know about.' So the disciples said to one another, 'Has anyone brought him something to eat?' Jesus said to them, 'My food is to do the will of him who sent me and to accomplish his work.'" (John 4:31-34)

Jesus knew that the work of the Kingdom was the only work that would last for eternity, and he was willing to say "no" to almost everything else.

Being a Gospel-centered man means saying "no" to the things that don't matter so that you can say "yes" to the things that do. Your first mission is to love Jesus and lead your family toward him, not to be the employee of the year. Work hard and work as if you are working for the Lord, but don't work so much that you neglect the titles that will last for eternity.

> *Your first mission
> is to love Jesus and
> lead your family
> toward him.*

WHAT'S ON YOUR MIND?

PRAYERS FOR YOUR WORK

_____

_____

_____

_____

_____

_____

_____

_____

_____

_____

_____

_____

_____

_____

_____

_____

_____

_____

_____

_____

_____

_____

PAID
MISSIONARIES

GO THEREFORE AND MAKE DISCIPLES OF ALL NATIONS, BAPTIZING THEM IN THE NAME OF THE FATHER AND OF THE SON AND OF THE HOLY SPIRIT, TEACHING THEM TO OBSERVE ALL THAT I HAVE COMMANDED YOU.

MATTHEW 28:19-20

#DadTired

When most Christians think of the "body of Christ," they think that there are paid professionals and then the rest of us.

I'll never forget when I was on staff at a church and I was talking to a member about how he engages his friends on the topic of Jesus. He jokingly said, "Well, isn't that what we pay you to do?"

...At least I hope he was joking.

The truth is, most Christians leave Jesus' command to "go and make disciples" for the pastors, missionaries, and evangelists to do. They feel ill-equipped to share the Gospel, and therefore leave that work for someone more qualified. They assume their job is no longer to make disciples, but rather, to invite their friends to church so that the professionals can convert them.

I don't think this is what Jesus had in mind.

What if I told you that you are a missionary? Not only that, but you are likely a paid missionary.

When translated correctly, Jesus' command to go and make disciples isn't about "going" as much as it is about "being." Jesus wasn't necessarily telling people to go and make disciples as much as he was telling people to make disciples as they go.

Some people go to the slums of Africa to share the Good News of Jesus. Some sneak into underground churches of China and preach the Gospel. Others pursue God's calling to pastor a church and equip other Christians for the work of ministry.

Most people will never live in Africa, China, or some other country. And even fewer people will sense God's call to pastor a church. But we are all called to make disciples as we go. Make no mistake about it—we are all called to be missionaries. We all have the same mission: to be used by God to see his Kingdom come to Earth as it is in Heaven.

This means that as you go about being the IT guy for your company, you are called to make disciples. As you sell homes in your community, you are called to make disciples. As you frame a house, flip a burger, manage an account, or run a tractor, you are called to make disciples.

What if instead of thinking about your job as a means to make money, you instead saw it as a way to get paid to share the Good News of the Gospel? Whether it's a government job, a Fortune 500 company, or a tiny mom and pop operation, God has planted you to be a missionary wherever you are, and the paycheck is just a bonus.

> *We all have the same mission: to be used by God to see his Kingdom come on Earth as it is in Heaven.*

WHAT'S ON YOUR MIND?

PRAYERS FOR YOUR WORK

WEEK FOUR // DAY SIX

GET TOGETHER

We'd love to see who you're meeting with. Post a picture of your group and use the hashtag **#DadTired**.

MEET WITH SOME FRIENDS OVER FOOD AND DRINK TO TALK ABOUT WHAT YOU LEARNED THIS WEEK. USE THESE QUESTIONS TO HELP KEEP THE CONVERSATION GOING.

Where are you currently finding your identity? If you lost your job today, where would your identity lie?

If you lost all your money tomorrow, would you have a hard time trusting in God as provider? Why or why not?

In what ways has money replaced God's role in your life?

What changes do you need to make to your schedule to better reflect what you value?

How would your work week look different if you saw yourself
as a paid missionary?

If you knew that you would never earn another dollar above what you
are currently making, how would your identity change in Christ?

REST

COME TO ME,
ALL WHO LABOR AND
ARE HEAVY LADEN,
AND I WILL GIVE YOU REST.
TAKE MY YOKE UPON YOU,
AND LEARN FROM ME,
FOR I AM GENTLE AND
LOWLY IN HEART,
AND YOU WILL FIND REST
FOR YOUR SOULS.
FOR MY YOKE IS EASY,
AND MY BURDEN IS LIGHT.

MATTHEW 11:28-30

WHAT'S ON YOUR MIND?

PRAYERS FOR YOUR WORK

FINAL THOUGHTS

God likes you. He doesn't just love you. He actually likes you. And it's not because of anything you've done.

I pray that this book was helpful in reminding you of that truth. I pray that you are so compelled by his love for you that you relentlessly chase after him, your wife, your kids, and his Kingdom. I pray that you set down the things that are distracting you from living out his mission and calling for your life. I pray that these words from 1 Timothy will be true for you as well:

"I have fought the good fight, I have finished the race, I have kept the faith." (1 Timothy 4:7)

I love you, brother. Now set this book down and go live it out.

Jerrad

WANT MORE?

WWW.DADTIRED.COM/PODCAST